The Bookshop
Strikes Back

Ann Patchett

B L O O M S B U R Y
LONDON · NEW DELHI · NEW YORK · SYDNEY

First published in Great Britain 2013

This essay first appeared in *Atlantic Monthly* and will also appear in
Ann Patchett's forthcoming book, *This Is the Story of a Happy Marriage*

Bloomsbury Publishing Plc
50 Bedford Square
London
WC1B 3DP

www.bloomsbury.com

Bloomsbury Publishing, London, New Delhi, New York and Sydney

A CIP catalogue record for this book is available from the British Library

ISBN 978 1 4088 4749 7

10 9 8 7 6 5 4 3 2 1

Typeset by seagulls.net

Printed in Great Britain by LDA, Berkshire

All papers used by Bloomsbury Publishing are natural, recyclable products
made from wood grown in well-managed forests. The manufacturing
processes conform to the environmental regulations of the country of origin.

IN LATE FEBRUARY of 2012 I am in my basement, which is really a very nice part of my house that is not done justice by the word *basement*. For the purposes of this story, let's call it the "Parnassus Fulfillment Center." I have hauled 533 boxed-up hardback copies of my latest novel, *State of Wonder*, from Parnassus, the bookstore I co-own in Nashville, into my car, driven them across town (three trips there, and three trips back), and then lugged them down here to the Parnassus Fulfillment Center. Along with the hardbacks, I have brought in countless paperback copies of my backlist books as well. I sign all these books, and stack them up on one enormous and extremely sturdy table. Then I call for backup: Patrik and Niki from the store, my friend Judy, my mother. Together we form an assembly line, taking the orders off the bookstore's website, addressing mailing labels, writing tiny thank-you notes to tuck inside the signed copies, then bubble-wrapping, taping, and packing them up to mail. We get a rhythm going, we have a system, and it's pretty smooth, except for removing the orders from the website. What I don't understand is that no matter how many orders I delete from the list, the list does not get smaller. We are all work and no progress, and I'm sure something must be going seriously wrong. After all, we've had this website for only a week, and who's to say we know what we're doing? "We know what we're doing," Niki says, and Patrik, who set up the website in the first place, confirms this. They explain to me that the reason the list isn't getting any shorter is that the orders are still coming in.

You may have heard the news that the independent bookstore is dead, that books are dead, that maybe even reading is dead – to which I say, Pull up a chair, friend. I have a story to tell.

The reason I am signing and wrapping books in my basement is that more orders have come in than the store can handle, and the reason so many orders have come in is that, a few days before, I had been a guest on *The Colbert Report*. After a healthy round of jousting about bookstores versus Amazon, Mr. Colbert held a copy of my novel in front of the cameras and exhorted America to buy it from Amazon – to which I, without a moment's thought (because *without a moment's thought* is how I fly these days) shouted, "No! No! Not Amazon. Order it off Parnassus Books dot net and I'll sign it for you." And America took me up on my offer, confirming once and for all that the Colbert Bump is real. That explains how I got stuck in the basement, but fails to answer the larger question: What was a writer of literary fiction whose "new" book was already ten months old doing on *The Colbert Report* in the first place? Hang on, because this is where things start to get weird: I was on the show not because I am a writer, but because I am a famous independent bookseller.

Let's go back to the beginning of the story.

A year before, the city of Nashville had two bookstores. One was Davis-Kidd, which had been our much-beloved locally owned and operated independent before selling out to the Ohio-based Joseph-Beth Booksellers chain ten years ago. Joseph-Beth moved Davis-Kidd into a mall, provided it with thirty thousand square feet of retail space, and put wind chimes and coffee mugs and scented candles in front of book displays. We continued to call it our "local independent," even though we knew it wasn't really true anymore. Nashville also had a Borders, which was about the same size as Davis-Kidd and sat on the edge of Vanderbilt's campus. (In candor, I should say that Nashville has some truly wonderful used-book stores that range from iconic to overwhelming. But while they play an important role in the cultural fabric of the city, it is a separate role – or maybe that's just the perspective of someone who writes books for a living. We have a Barnes & Noble that is a twenty-minute drive out of town if traffic is light, a Books-a-Million on the western edge of the city near a Costco, and a Target that also sell books. Do those count? Not to me, no, they don't, and they don't count to any other book-buying Nashvillians with whom I am acquainted.)

In December 2010, Davis-Kidd closed. It had been profitable, declared the owners from Ohio who were dismantling the chain, but not profitable enough. Then, in March 2011, our Borders store – also profitable – went the way of all Borders stores. We woke up one morning and found we no longer had a bookstore.

How had this happened? Had digital books led us astray? Had we been lured away by the siren song of Amazon's undercut pricing? Had we been careless, failed to support the very places that had hosted our children's story hours and brought in touring authors and set up summer-reading tables? Our city experienced a great collective gnashing of teeth and rending of garments, but to what extent was Nashville to blame? *Both of the closed stores had been profitable.* Despite the fact that our two bookstores were the size of small department stores and bore enormous rents, they had been making their numbers every month. Nashvillians, I'd like the record to show, had been buying books.

The Nashville Public Library organized community forums for concerned citizens to come together and discuss how we might get a bookstore again. Our library, and I will bless them forever, immediately jumped up to fill the void, hosting readings of orphaned authors whose tours had already been scheduled to include trips to Nashville (including mine), and in every way trying to responsibly tackle the problems we faced as a city in need of a bookstore. Someone went so far as to suggest putting a little bookstore in the library, though selling books in the same building where books were free struck me as a bad plan. Surely, I thought, *someone* would open a bookstore.

My secret was that I did not much miss those mall-sized Gargantuas. The store I really missed had been gone much longer than they had. Mills was the bookstore of my youth. My sister and I used to walk there every day after school, stopping first to check out the puppies in the pet shop across the street, and then going on to admire the glossy covers of the Kristin Lavransdatter series, which is what girls read after they had finished the *Little House* books, back before the *Twilight* books were written. Mills could not have been more than seven hundred square feet small, and the people who worked there remembered who you were and what you read, even if you were ten. If I could have that kind of bookstore, one that valued books and readers above muffins and adorable plastic watering cans, a store that recognized it could not possibly stock every single book that every single person might be looking for, and so stocked the books the staff had read and liked and could recommend, if I could re-create the bookish happiness of my childhood, then maybe *I* was the person for the job. Or maybe not. I wanted to go into retail about as much as I wanted to go into the army.

"You're like a really good cook who thinks she should open a restaurant," my friend Steve Turner told me over dinner. I had gone to Steve for advice, because he has a particular knack for starting businesses, which has led to his knack for making money. He was trying to talk me down from the ledge. "And anyway, you already have a job."

"I wasn't thinking of working in the bookstore," I said.

He shook his head. "Don't ever think you can start a business and just turn it over to someone else. It never works."

In truth, I left that dinner feeling relieved. I'd been to the oracle and the oracle had told me that mine was a bad idea, which must have been what I'd wanted to hear.

In fact, it was exactly Steve Turner's admonition I was thinking of when I met Karen Hayes the next week. We were introduced by our one friend in common, Mary Grey James. Karen was then a sales rep for Random House, and Mary Grey had been a rep for Harcourt. They had both worked at Ingram, a large book distributor outside of Nashville. Karen, who is tall and pale and very serious in a way that brings pilgrims or homesteaders or other indefatigably hardworking people to mind, meant to open a bookstore. Her plan was to quit her job and devote her life to the project. All she lacked was the money. I suggested, having never considering investing in the book business, and not having been asked to do so, that I could pay for the store and promote it. Karen and I would be co-owners, and Mary Grey would be the store's general manager, thus solving the problem of how I could have a bookstore without having to actually work in a bookstore. We hammered out a tentative plan in the time it took to eat our sandwiches. Then Karen pulled a prospectus out of her bag and handed it to me.

"It's called Parnassus Books," she said.

I looked at the word, which struck me as hard to spell and harder to remember. I shook my head. "I don't like it," I said. How many people would know what it meant? (In Greek mythology, Mount Parnassus is the home of literature, learning, and music, and, I think, a few other valuable things.) I had wanted a store called Independent People, after the great Halldór Laxness novel about Iceland and sheep, or perhaps Red Bird Books, as I believed that simple titles, especially those containing colors, were memorable.

"I've always wanted a bookstore called Parnassus," Karen said.

I looked at this woman I didn't know, my potential business partner. I wanted a bookstore in Nashville. Why should I get to name it? "You're the one who's going to work there," I told her.

That night, after talking it over with my husband and then securing a more detailed character reference from Mary Grey, I called Karen. According to her numbers, three hundred thousand dollars would be needed to open a twenty-five-hundred-square-foot bookstore. I told her I was in. This was on April 30th, 2011; in two weeks, I was to leave for the U.K. leg of the *State of Wonder* book tour. The U.S. leg of the tour started June 7th. Karen was working for Random House until

June 10th. "Should I announce this on book tour?" I asked her. I knew I'd be giving interviews all day long during the entire month of June. Should I tell people what we had planned over lunch? That we had a name I didn't like but money in the bank, that we were strangers?

"Sure," Karen said, after some real hesitation. "I guess."

When I look back on all this now I'm dizzied by the blitheness that stood in place of any sort of business sense, the grand gesture of walking over to the roulette table and betting it all on a single number. Anyone I mentioned this plan to was quick to remind me that books were dead, that in two years – I have no idea where "two years" came from, but that figure was consistently thrown at me – books would no longer exist, much less bookstores, and that I might as well be selling eight-track tapes and typewriters. But somehow all the naysaying never lodged itself in my brain. I could see it working as clearly as I could see me standing beside my sister in Mills. I was a writer, after all, and my books sold pretty well. I spoke to crowds of enthusiastic readers all over the country, and those readers were my proof. More than that, I was partnered with Karen Hayes, who wore the steely determination of a woman who could clear a field and plant it herself; and with Mary Grey, my dear friend who had opened a bookstore before. Moreover, our two giant, departed bookstores had been profitable every month; there was the roulette ball bouncing up again and again until finally coming to rest on the number I had chosen.

I would leave soon on my U.S. tour, but Karen and I managed to look at some possible spaces. We were like a couple of newlyweds in an arranged marriage looking for our first apartment. We didn't know what the other one would like, and our conversations were awkward exchanges followed by long periods of awkward silence. One place had only studded two-by-fours for walls, a forlorn toilet lying on its side in the center of the dark room. Karen could see the potential. (Karen, it quickly became clear, has a much greater capacity for seeing potential than I have.) She saw it again in a restaurant space that had been empty for four years. We picked our way carefully towards the kitchen, letting the beams from our flashlights slide over grease-covered refrigerators and stoves. I had eaten in this place as a child, and it was disgusting even then. It was also huge. "Maybe we could partner with someone who wanted to start a cooking school," Karen said, looking at the hulking appliances. We were open to all possibilities. I was certain that some of the men who showed us these spaces had failed to secure bit parts on *The Sopranos* or in *Glengarry Glen Ross* but were still practicing for the roles. Often I was grateful for the lack of electricity, certain I would see things in those rooms I didn't want to see. I wanted someplace whistle-clean and move-in ready, preferably with built-in cherry shelving. Karen, however, was in the market for cheap. The place we both favored had once been a sushi restaurant and now had a lien against it. When the manager finally got around to giving us an answer, it was a pronouncement that bookstores were dead and that he wouldn't rent to us at any price.

And so, without a location or anything like an opening date, I left for my book tour, and on the first day announced on *The Diane Rehm Show* that, along with my partner, Karen Hayes, I would be opening an independent bookstore in Nashville. I was vague on every detail, but when asked about the name, I managed to say "Parnassus."

Early in the tour I got a phone call from The Beveled Edge, the frame shop in Nashville where I had long done business. They asked if I wanted them to sell my new book. My alterations shop, Stitch-It, followed suit. I was extremely grateful to be able to tell people in my hometown where they could go to find my novel, but the experience made me feel the loss of a real bookstore more acutely. Parnassus was a good idea for Nashville, yes, but selling books was also in my own best interest.

State of Wonder was my sixth novel and eighth book, and while I've been on many book tours, this one brought with it an entirely new sense of purpose. I was going out to bookstores to read and sign, sure, but I was also there to learn. I wanted to know how many square feet each store had, and how many part-time employees, and where they got those good-looking greeting cards. Booksellers do not guard their best secrets: they are a generous tribe and were quick to welcome me into their fold and to give me advice. I was told to hang merchandise from the ceiling whenever possible, because people long to buy whatever requires a ladder to cut it down. The children's section should always be in a back corner of the store, so that when parents inevitably wandered off and started reading, their offspring could be caught before they busted out of the store. I received advice about bookkeeping, bonuses, staff recommendations, and websites.

While I was flying from city to city, Karen was driving around the South in a U-haul, buying up shelving at rock-bottom prices from various Borders stores that were liquidating.

I had written one check before I left, for a hundred and fifty thousand dollars, and I kept asking if she needed more money. No, she didn't need more money.

At the end of the summer, Karen and I finally settled on a former tanning salon a few doors down from a doughnut shop and a nail emporium. Unlike the property managers we had encountered earlier in our quest, the one responsible for this location was a business-savvy Buddhist who felt a bookstore would lend class to his L-shaped strip mall, and to this end was willing to foot the bill to have the tile floors chipped out. The space was long and deep, with ceilings that were too high for us to ever dream of hanging things from. The tanning beds were carted away, but the sign over the door stayed up for a ridiculously long time: TAN 2000. I went to Australia on yet another leg of my book tour, leaving all the work on Karen's head.

The word had spread to the Southern Hemisphere. In Australia, all anyone wanted to talk about was the bookstore. Journalists were calling from Germany and India, wanting to talk about the bookstore. Every interview started off the same way: Hadn't I heard the news? Had no one thought to tell me? Bookstores were over. Then, one by one, the interviewers recounted the details of their own favorite stores, and I listened. They told me, confidentially and off the record, that they thought I just might succeed.

I was starting to understand the role the interviews would play in that success. In my thirties, I had paid my rent by writing for fashion magazines. I found *Elle* to be the most baffling because its editors insisted on identifying trends. Since most fashion magazines "closed" (industry jargon for the point at which the pages are shipped to the printing plant) three months before they hit the newsstands, the identification of trends, especially from Nashville, required an act of near clairvoyance. Eventually, I realized what everyone in fashion already knew: a trend is whatever you call a trend. *This spring in Paris, fashionistas will wear fishbowls on their heads*. In my hotel room in Australia, this insight came back to me more as a vision than as a memory. "The small independent bookstore is coming back," I told reporters in Berlin and Bangladesh. "It's part of a trend."

My act was on the road, and with every performance I tweaked the script, hammering out the details as I proclaimed them to strangers: all things happen in a cycle, I explained – the little bookstore had succeeded and grown into a bigger bookstore. Seeing the potential for profit, the superstore chains rose up and crushed the independents, then Amazon rose up and crushed the superstore chains. Now that we could order any book at any hour without having to leave the screen in front of us, we realized what we had lost: the community center, the human interaction, the recommendation of a smart reader rather than a computer algorithm telling us what other shoppers had purchased. I promised whomever was listening that from those very ashes the small independent bookstore would rise again.

What about the e-books, the journalists wanted to know. How can you survive the e-books?

And so I told them – I care *that* you read, not *how* you read. Most independent bookstores, and certainly Barnes & Noble, are capable of selling e-books through their websites, and those e-books can be downloaded onto any e-reader except for Amazon's Kindle, which worked only for Amazon purchases. So you can support a bookstore in your community and still read a book on your iPad.

Say it enough times and it will be true.

Build it and they will come.

In Melbourne, I gave a reading with Jonathan Franzen. I asked him if he would come to the bookstore. Sure, he said,

he'd like to do that. Down in the Antipodes, my mind began to
flip through my Rolodex. I know a lot of writers.

Meanwhile, back in Nashville, Karen and Mary Grey had hired
a staff, and together they washed the warehoused Borders
bookshelves again and again while they waited for the paint to
dry and the new flooring to arrive. In a burst of optimism, we
had hoped to open October 1st. Lights were still missing when
we finally did open on November 15th. We had forgotten to
get cash for the cash register, and I ran to the bank with my
checkbook. That morning, the *New York Times* ran a story about
the opening of Parnassus, along with a photo of me, on page A1.

Imagine a group of highly paid consultants crowded into
the offices of my publisher, HarperCollins. Their job is to try
and figure out how to get a picture of a literary novelist (me,
say) on the front page of the *Times*. "She could kill someone,"
one consultant suggests. The other consultants shake their
heads. "It would have to be someone very famous," another
says. "Could she hijack a busload of school children, or maybe
restructure the New York public school system?" They sigh. It
would not be enough. They run down a list of crimes, stunts,
and heroically good deeds, but none of them are Page One

material. I can promise you this: kept in that room for all eternity, they would not have landed on the idea that opening a twenty-five-hundred-square-foot bookstore in Nashville would do the trick.

The bookstore that does in fact open in Nashville is so beautiful I can't even make sense of it. While I've spent the summer talking, Karen has taken her dreams out of the air. She has made the ideal bookstore of her own imagination into a place where you can actually come and buy books. I realize now my business partner is something of a novelist herself. She attended to the most tedious details, and then went on to make a work of art. Through every color choice, every cabinet, every twinkling hanging star, she had conjured a world that was worth inexpressibly more than the sum of its dazzling parts, the kind of bookstore children will remember when they are old themselves. Parnassus, I could finally see, was perfectly named, as she had known all along it would be. Every time I walk through the door I think, Karen was the one person I met who wanted to open a bookstore, and how did I have the sense upon meeting her to sign on for life?

On opening day, National Public Radio wanted an interview from the store. They wanted background noise, but too many people made too much background noise and we had to retreat to the back corner of the storage room. Then *CBS This Morning* called at four o'clock that afternoon. I would have to get on a plane in the next two hours to be on CBS in the morning. When we had our grand opening the following Saturday, an all-day extravaganza that stretched from early-morning puppet shows to late-night wine and cheese, an estimated three thousand Nashvillians came through the store, devouring books like locusts sweeping through a field of summer wheat. All of us who worked there (not a number I normally include myself in, but in this case I was among them) had waited so long for customers that once they finally came we could not stop telling them what we wanted them to read. One more joy I had failed to consider: that I can talk strangers into reading books that I love. The shelves we had so recently washed and dried and loaded down were startlingly empty. Karen kept running back to the office to order yet more books, while I kept climbing onto a bench to make yet another speech. Every local television news program came, every local newspaper, along with *People* magazine. I was interviewed so many times a person walking past the window of our bookstore on his way to the Donut

Den might think that we had won the Derby, or cured cancer, or found a portal to the South Pole.

"You know," I had told Karen early on, "you're going to wind up doing all the work and I'm going to get all the credit. That could get really annoying."

But she didn't seem annoyed, either by the abstract concept or, later, by the omnipresent and unavoidable reality. "You just do your job," she told me. "I'll do mine." My job has become something I could never have imagined, and while it surely benefits Parnassus, Parnassus is not exactly the point. Without ever knowing that such a position existed, let alone that it might be available, I have inadvertently become the spokesperson for independent bookstores. People still want books; I've got the numbers to prove it. I imagine they remember the bookstores of their own youth with the same tenderness that I remember mine. They are lined up outside most mornings when we open our doors because, I think, they have learned through this journey we've all been on that the lowest price is not always the best value. Parnassus Books creates jobs in our community and contributes to the tax base. We've made a place to bring children to learn and to play, and to think those two things are one and the same. We have a piano. We have a dachshund.

We have authors who come and read, and you can ask them questions, and they will sign your book. The business model may be antiquated, but it's the one that I like, and so far it's the one that's working.

And maybe it's working because I'm an author, and maybe it's working because Karen works like life depends on this bookstore, or because we have a particularly brilliant staff, or because Nashville is a city that is particularly sympathetic to all things independent. Maybe we just got lucky. But my luck has made me believe that changing the course of the corporate world is possible. Amazon doesn't get to make all the decisions; the people can make them by how and where they spend their money. If what a bookstore offers matters to you, then shop at a bookstore. If you feel that the experience of reading a book is valuable, then read the book. This is how we change the world: we grab hold of it. We change ourselves.

(*Atlantic Monthly*, November 2012 and taken from the forthcoming book *This Is the Story of a Happy Marriage*, published by Bloomsbury 7 November 2013)

A NOTE ON THE AUTHOR

ANN PATCHETT is the author of six novels including *Run* and *Bel Canto*, and three works of non-fiction. She has been shortlisted for the Orange Prize for Fiction three times; with *The Magician's Assistant* in 1998, winning the prize with *Bel Canto* in 2002, and was most recently shortlisted with *State of Wonder* in 2012. She writes for the *New York Times Magazine*, *Elle*, *GQ*, the *Financial Times*, the *Paris Review* and *Vogue*. She lives in Nashville, Tennessee.